D0773417

How to Analyze the Films of

CLINT
EASTWOOD

by Casie Hermansson

ABDO
Publishing Company

Essential Critiques

CLINT
EASTWOOD

by Casie Hermansson

Content Consultant: Dr. Walter C. Metz, Professor and Chair
Department of Cinema and Photography
Southern Illinois University Carbondale

Credits

Published by ABDO Publishing Company, PO Box 398166, Minneapolis, MN 55439. Copyright © 2013 by Abdo Consulting Group, Inc. International copyrights reserved in all countries. No part of this book may be reproduced in any form without written permission from the publisher. The Essential Library™ is a trademark and logo of ABDO Publishing Company.

Printed in the United States of America,
North Mankato, Minnesota
062012
092012

♻ THIS BOOK CONTAINS AT LEAST 10% RECYCLED MATERIALS.

Editor: Lauren Coss
Series Designer: Marie Tupy

Library of Congress Cataloging-in-Publication Data
Hermansson, Casie.
  How to analyze the films of Clint Eastwood / Casie Hermansson.
     p. cm. -- (Essential critiques)
  Includes bibliographical references.
  ISBN 978-1-61783-453-0
  1. Eastwood, Clint, 1930---Criticism and interpretation--Juvenile literature. 2. Film criticism--Juvenile literature. I. Title.
  PN2287.E37H47 2013
  791.4302'33092--dc22

                          2012016737

Table of Contents

Introduction to Critiques

What Is Critical Theory?

What do you usually do as a member of an audience watching a movie? You probably enjoy the settings, the costumes, and the sound track. You learn about the characters as they are developed through dialogue and other interactions. You might be drawn in by the plot of the movie, eager to find out what happens next. Yet these are only a few of many ways of understanding and appreciating a movie. What if you are interested in delving more deeply? You might want to learn more about the director and how his or her personal background is reflected in the film. Or you might want to examine what the film says about society—how it depicts the roles of women and minorities, for example. If so, you have entered the realm of critical theory.

Critical theory helps you learn how various works of art, literature, music, theater, film, and other endeavors either support or challenge the way society behaves. Critical theory is the evaluation and interpretation of a work using different philosophies, or schools of thought. Critical theory can be used to understand all types of cultural productions.

There are many different critical theories. If you are analyzing a movie, each theory asks you to look at the work from a different perspective. Some theories address social issues, while others focus on the director's life, what role the direction plays in the overall film, or the time period in which the film was written or set. For example, the critical theory that asks how a director's life and filmmaking style affected the work is called auteur criticism. Other common, broad schools of criticism include historical criticism, feminist criticism, and ideological criticism.

What Is the Purpose of Critical Theory?

Critical theory can open your mind to new ways of thinking. It can help you evaluate a movie from a new perspective, directing your attention to issues and messages you may not otherwise recognize in a work. For example, applying feminist criticism to a film may make you aware of female stereotypes perpetuated in the work. Applying a critical theory to a work helps you learn about the person who created it or the society that enjoyed it. You can explore how the movie is perceived by current cultures.

How Do You Apply Critical Theory?

You conduct a critique when you use a critical theory to examine and question a work. The theory you choose is a lens through which you can view the work, or a springboard for asking questions about the work. Applying a critical theory helps you to think critically about the work. You are free to question the work and make an assertion about it. If you choose to examine a film using auteur theory, for example, you want to know how the director's personal background, education, or filmmaking techniques inspired or shaped the work. You could explore why the director was drawn to the story. For instance, are there any parallels between a particular character's life and the director's life?

Forming a Thesis

Ask your question and find answers in the work or other related materials. Then you can create a thesis. The thesis is the key point in your critique. It is your argument about the work based on the tenets, or beliefs, of the theory you are using. For example, if you are using auteur theory to ask how the director's life inspired the work, your thesis could be worded as follows: Director Teng Xiong, raised in refugee camps in Southeast Asia, drew upon her experiences to direct the movie *No Home for Me*.

> How to Make
> a Thesis Statement
>
> In a critique, a thesis statement typically appears at the end of the introductory paragraph. It is usually only one sentence long and states the author's main idea.

Providing Evidence

Once you have formed a thesis, you must provide evidence to support it. Evidence might take the form of examples and quotations from the work itself—such as dialogue from a film. Articles about the movie or personal interviews with the director might also support your ideas. You may wish to address what other critics have written about the work. Quotes from these individuals may help support your claim. If you find any quotes or examples that contradict your thesis, you will need to create an argument against them.

For instance: Many critics have pointed to the heroine of No Home for Me as a powerless victim of circumstances. However, through her dialogue and strong actions, she is clearly depicted as someone who seeks to shape her own future.

> ### How to Support a Thesis Statement
>
> A critique should include several arguments. Arguments support a thesis claim. An argument is one or two sentences long and is supported by evidence from the work being discussed.
>
> Organize the arguments into paragraphs. These paragraphs make up the body of the critique.

In This Book

In this book, you will read overviews of famous movies by director Clint Eastwood, each followed by a critique. Each critique will use one theory and apply it to one work. Critical thinking sections will give you a chance to consider other theses and questions about the work. Did you agree with the author's application of the theory? What other questions are raised by the thesis and its arguments? You can also find out what other critics think about each particular film. Then, in the You Critique It section in the final pages of this book, you will have an opportunity to create your own critique.

Look for the Guides

Throughout the chapters that analyze the works, thesis statements have been highlighted. The box next to the thesis helps explain what questions are being raised about the work. Supporting arguments have been underlined. The boxes next to the arguments help explain how these points support the thesis. Look for these guides throughout each critique.

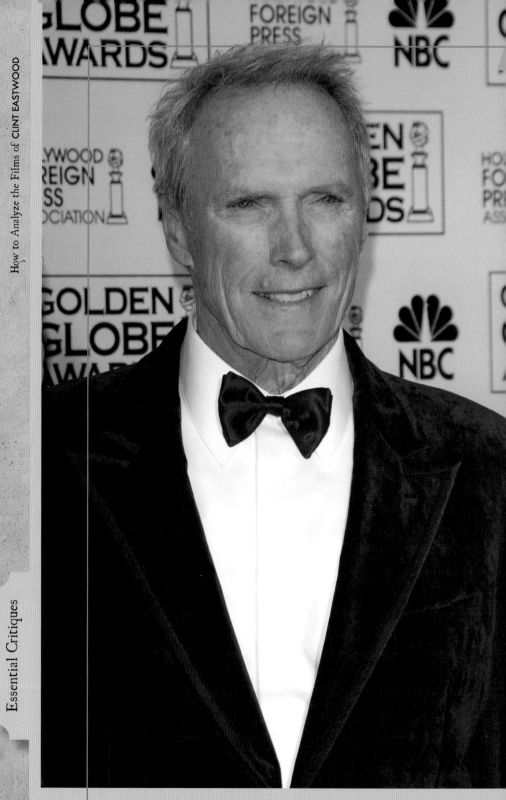

Actor and director Clint Eastwood has been considered one of the most talented in his field since his career took off in the 1960s.

2

A Closer Look at Clint Eastwood

Clint Eastwood is a respected Hollywood veteran on both sides of the camera. He has won Academy Awards for directing. It is hard to believe that as a young man Eastwood showed more promise as a musician, a swimmer, or even an aircraft technician than he did as an actor. Even when he began taking drama classes he had little desire to perform, and his teachers saw nothing special. However, since then, Eastwood has become an icon of US film and filmmaking.

A Roving Childhood

Clinton Eastwood Jr. was born on May 31, 1930, in San Francisco, California, to a musical mother, Margaret Ruth Renner, and an athletic father, Clinton Eastwood Sr. Clint's younger sister,

Jeanne, was born in 1934. Clinton Sr. had worked as a salesman. However, the Great Depression triggered by the 1929 stock market crash took him and his young family up and down the West Coast looking for work. Although Clint remembers his family always had a positive attitude, he often felt lonely as a young boy.

This rootless life ended for a time in 1940 when Clint was ten. His father found permanent work and bought a house in San Francisco's East Bay Area. The Eastwoods stayed there for the next eight years. Clint attended Havens Elementary and Piedmont Junior High School, where he formed lifelong friendships.

Clint was extremely shy as a child. Though he was a talented athlete and musician, he preferred not to display his skills publicly. When Clint was in eighth grade, he participated in his first school play. His English teacher had to force him to take the lead role. However, he enjoyed watching films and even sneaked into movie theaters to see movies.

Clinton Sr. taught his son the value of hard work, and Clint had various jobs before and after school. He worked outdoors during summer vacations, doing odd jobs such as baling hay,

Though Clint struggled in school, he graduated from Oakland Technical High School in 1949.

cutting timber, and delivering newspapers. Clint was a hard worker, but he struggled academically. Eventually, the Eastwoods decided Clint might be better suited to a different learning environment. He attended Oakland Technical High School, where he studied aircraft maintenance. He was already familiar with the inner workings of cars and carried this knowledge over to his new school. Even though he was attending a technical school, Clint's interest in music did not waver. He became obsessed with jazz music in late high school, an interest that would become a lifelong passion.

During Clint's senior year of high school, his family moved to Seattle, Washington. However, Clint finished high school in California, joining his family in Seattle for a short time after graduating in 1949. After graduation, Clint moved from place to place, even giving up music during this time; he now calls these his "lost years."[1] In 1951, as he was deciding whether to go to college to study music, he was drafted for the Korean War (1950–1953).

Sink or Swim

While in the army, Eastwood was sent to basic training at Fort Ord in Monterey Bay, California. While in training, Eastwood caught a ride on a navy plane to visit his family in Seattle for the weekend. On the return trip, the plane crashed into the cold waters of San Francisco Bay. Eastwood survived the crash and swam more than a mile through jellyfish- and shark-infested waters to reach shore.

After two years serving as a swim instructor for the army, Eastwood signed up for a business program at Los Angeles City College in Los Angeles, California, in 1953. He worked as a gas station attendant, among other odd jobs, to support himself. Although Eastwood was studying business, he also began taking drama classes. In Los Angeles, Eastwood met and began dating Maggie Johnson. They married on December 19, 1953.

Actor for Hire

Eastwood was recruited from the drama group he was a part of to join a group of contract players, or paid actors, for Universal Studios in the mid-1950s. Universal employed these actors as a pool of talent it could choose from when making movies. The actors attended classes more than five days a week on topics including acting, speaking, singing, dancing, and horseback riding. Eastwood was given a six-month contract. Though he was known for his good looks, he worked hard to improve his acting skills during this time. His first part was a lab assistant in a scene in the horror film sequel *Revenge of the Creature*. Eastwood later admitted to flubbing his few lines twice before getting them right. The film was released in 1955. Eastwood got a few more roles, and his position as a contract player was renewed. However, Universal ended the contract in October 1955.

Although he was not hired elsewhere as a contract player, Eastwood got small parts and some recurring roles on television shows. Even with these paid acting roles, money was tight. Eastwood worked weekends digging swimming pools to make ends meet.

Rawhide Cowboy and the Spaghetti Westerns

Eastwood came to fame in 1959 as the cowboy Rowdy Yates in a new television series titled *Rawhide*. The show became very popular and ran until 1966. *Rawhide* was an excellent learning experience for Eastwood. Over the course of more than 200 episodes, he had the opportunity to observe many established actors as they came on set to do guest appearances. The recurring role also gave Eastwood the job security to experiment with his acting. Because television shows often have multiple directors, Eastwood had the chance to observe many directors—good and bad—at work behind the camera. He learned what worked and what did not in directing, and he even directed some trailers for the show.

After six years as Rowdy, Eastwood said he had "nothing to lose" when he was invited to join director Sergio Leone in Spain and Rome, Italy, to shoot a Western film.[2] It would be the first of three Westerns the two men would make together: *A Fistful of Dollars* (1964), *For a Few Dollars More* (1965), and *The Good, the Bad and the Ugly* (1966). Leone did not speak English, and Eastwood did not speak Italian, the language of Leone and the cast. Leone gave Eastwood the opportunity to rewrite the script, and he became more involved in the production of the three films than had been permitted on *Rawhide*. Eastwood had fun with the projects, but when the films were released in the United States, the style of these Westerns was so foreign that a new name was made for them: the spaghetti Western.

In 1966, *Rawhide* ended. But Eastwood's acting career was just beginning. He soon found himself with a steady stream of film work from a number of directors. He began displaying a new confidence and maturity in his acting. He was often cast in a strong and silent role in Westerns, and he became so well known in this genre he had to remind one reporter, "I'm an actor, you know, not a *real* cowboy."[3] When Eastwood was paired with star Richard Burton for the World War II–era action film *Where Eagles Dare*, he was famous enough for MGM Studios to bank on audiences seeing the film simply because Eastwood was in it. The film became MGM's biggest hit of 1969.

Eastwood was becoming a household name, but the 1971 film *Dirty Harry* launched him into superstardom. Eastwood played "Dirty" Harry Callahan, a San Francisco detective engaged in a war of wits with a serial killer. Dirty Harry's line to a street criminal, "You've gotta ask yourself a question. Do I feel lucky? Well do ya, punk?" has been called the most famous Eastwood line on film.[4] The film was extremely violent, and its violence caused a lot of discussion in the press and the film community. However, Eastwood has always defended his character and the film. *Dirty Harry* was hugely successful, and in the four sequels that followed, Eastwood learned a lot about filming fast action sequences from the film's director, Don Siegel. Eastwood himself even directed one of the action sequences.

Eastwood the Director

In 1967, Eastwood had formed his own production company, which he named Malpaso. The first Malpaso production was the Western *Hang 'Em High*, released in 1968. Malpaso produced or coproduced many of Eastwood's films. As a result, Eastwood maintained enormous control over all aspects of his films.

Eastwood made his debut as a director with the suspense film *Play Misty for Me*, released in 1971. In 1985, Eastwood directed the Western *Pale Rider*, which he also starred in. He liked to keep the same cast and crew as much as possible for the films he directed. By the time Eastwood directed *Unforgiven*, which won four Oscars at the 1993 Academy Awards, including Best Director and Best Picture, many of the crew members had worked with him for more than 20 years.

Though Eastwood's film career was going well, his personal life was never quite as smooth. Eastwood and Maggie separated in 1979. They divorced in 1984. In addition to two children with Maggie, Eastwood had five other children, including a daughter with his second wife, Dina Ruiz, whom he married in 1996.

Despite these personal transitions, Eastwood's directing credentials continued growing. In 2004, he was nominated for the Academy Award for Best Director for the 2003 film *Mystic River*, starring well-known actors Sean Penn and Tim Robbins. Eastwood both directed and starred in the 2004 film *Million Dollar Baby*, for which he won the 2005 Academy Awards for Best Picture and Best Director. Hilary Swank won the Academy Award for Best Actress for her role in the film.

Eastwood also directed and starred in the 2008 film *Gran Torino*. Though it was not nominated for an Academy Award, the film garnered much critical acclaim and showed Eastwood's depth as both an actor and a director. In 2011, *J. Edgar* was released. Eastwood directed the film, which focuses on the life of J. Edgar Hoover, the director of the Federal Bureau of Investigation (FBI) from the 1930s to the 1970s. Although he claimed his part in *Gran Torino* would be his last acting role, in late 2011, the 81-year-old Eastwood agreed to appear in *Trouble with the Curve* in the role of an aging baseball scout. The movie began filming in early 2012 and was scheduled for release later that year.

Eastwood accepted his first Academy Award in 1993 when he won Best Director for his work on *Unforgiven*, which also won Best Picture.

Eastwood's long and successful career is a testimony to his hard work ethic. Like his mentor Siegel, Eastwood is a generous director and is always open to hearing how a shot could be improved. As both an actor and a director, he strives to learn from everyone around him, and audiences around the world reap the benefits of his hard work when they watch his masterful films.

In *Dirty Harry*, Eastwood stars as Police Inspector Harry Callahan, a determined San Francisco cop with little regard for the rules.

An Overview
of *Dirty Harry*

San Francisco in Peril

Dirty Harry opens with a dramatic scene of a sniper on a San Francisco rooftop shooting a female swimmer. Police Inspector Harry Callahan, played by Eastwood, investigates the murder and finds a note left by the killer. In the note, the killer says he wants $100,000, or he will kill again. He says next time he will kill either a Catholic priest or an African American. The letter is signed "Scorpio."

Callahan is a loner whose wife was killed in a car accident several years ago. He resents authority and is constantly at odds with his superiors. He has little regard for rules and will do what it takes to get his job done. Later, as he is eating a hot dog across the street from a bank, Callahan notices a bank robbery in progress. He shoots several robbers as they try to escape and is shot in the leg in the process. He aims his gun—a .44 Magnum, which only has six shots—at one robber lying in the bank doorway. Callahan says he cannot remember if he has any bullets left. He asks if the man feels lucky, and the robber surrenders. Callahan's gun is empty.

Lieutenant Al Bressler congratulates Callahan on stopping the robbery and informs him he is being given a partner. Bressler introduces Callahan to his new partner, Chico Gonzalez, who attended college and is of Mexican descent. Callahan does not want a partner; he believes himself to be bad luck. One of Callahan's former partners was killed, and his current partner is recovering from a gunshot wound. Another cop, Frank DiGiorgio, tells Gonzalez that Callahan hates everybody. Callahan tells Gonzalez he especially hates Mexicans. He also warns Gonzalez, "Just don't let your college degree get you killed."[1]

The Hunt for Scorpio

The police are using helicopters to watch rooftops across the city, and they interrupt Scorpio as he is taking aim at a young African-American man. Scorpio escapes. That night, as they are driving through the city, Callahan and Gonzalez

think they see someone matching Scorpio's description. They track the man to an apartment building. Peering through the window, Callahan realizes the man is not Scorpio, but then locals attack Callahan, believing he is a Peeping Tom. When Gonzalez arrives to rescue him, Callahan tells him not to arrest the men.

Callahan and Gonzalez are then called to stop a suicide attempt, and Callahan is sent up to the rooftop to help the suicidal man. On the roof, Callahan teases the man until he lunges to attack, and they are then lowered safely to the ground.

Loner Callahan has no interest in a partner when Al Bressler assigns him Chico Gonzalez, *center*.

Callahan tells Gonzalez he earned his nickname because he gets "every dirty job that comes along."[2]

Scorpio strikes again, killing a young African-American child. Hoping Scorpio will use the same rooftop he used before, near a Catholic church, Callahan and Gonzalez stake out the rooftop. Callahan gets distracted and misses Scorpio's arrival. Callahan fires at Scorpio but misses. Scorpio fires a machine gun at Callahan and Gonzalez and laughs. He misses both men but destroys their spotlight so they can no longer see him.

The next day, Lieutenant Bressler tells Callahan and Gonzalez that Scorpio has abducted a 14-year-old girl. Scorpio sends the police her underwear, one of her teeth, and a ransom note saying she has been buried alive with enough air to survive until early the next morning. The police want to pay the ransom and decide Callahan will take the bag of money to the drop-off point. However, Scorpio is not at the drop-off point, and he sends Callahan on a wild goose chase all over the city. Scorpio calls pay phones, sending Callahan from place to place to make sure he is not being followed. Callahan has a microphone taped under his shirt, so Gonzalez can listen in and follow Callahan from a safe distance.

When Callahan finally meets Scorpio in a city park, Scorpio tells him he plans to let the girl die, and he plans to kill Callahan as well. He begins beating Callahan. Gonzalez arrives just in time to shoot at Scorpio. He misses, and Scorpio shoots him in the chest. Callahan stabs Scorpio in the thigh with a knife he has taped to his ankle. Scorpio escapes. Both Callahan and Gonzalez survive their injuries.

The police get a call from an emergency room doctor who reports he has treated a man with a stab wound in the leg. Callahan and DiGiorgio go to the hospital, where the doctor tells them he has seen the man—Scorpio—before at a nearby stadium. Callahan and DiGiorgio go to the stadium to find Scorpio. Callahan chases Scorpio through the stadium while DiGiorgio tries to turn on the lights. Callahan catches the injured Scorpio and hurts him until he reveals where the girl is. Police find her dead. However, because Callahan entered the stadium illegally, when the police find the girl they cannot charge Scorpio with the murder. Callahan is furious, so he tails Scorpio everywhere, making it impossible for Scorpio to kill again. Scorpio pays someone to beat him up and claims it was Callahan who did it.

Callahan Goes Rogue

Callahan visits Gonzalez in the hospital, where Gonzalez tells him he is going to quit the police force to become a teacher. Gonzalez's wife asks Callahan how his wife can stand having him in the police force; Callahan tells her his wife was killed by a drunk driver.

Scorpio steals a gun and hijacks a school bus with seven children and the driver on board. The mayor gives his word of honor that Scorpio will get the ransom he asks for, but Callahan takes matters into his own hands. He waits for the bus and jumps onto its roof. Scorpio drives into a quarry where the final shootout occurs. Scorpio takes one last hostage, a boy fishing in the lake, but Callahan shoots Scorpio in the shoulder, and the boy escapes. Callahan aims his gun at Scorpio again, saying:

> *I know what you're thinking, punk. You're thinking, did he fire six shots or only five? Now, to tell you the truth, I forgot myself in all this excitement. But being this is a .44 Magnum, the most powerful handgun in the world and will blow your head clean off, you've gotta ask yourself a question. Do I feel lucky? Well do ya, punk?[3]*

Scorpio reaches for his weapon; Callahan kills him. Callahan throws his police badge into the lake and walks away.

Scorpio reaches for his gun, but Callahan shoots him just in time.

Harry Callahan embodies the macho characteristics Eastwood is famous for portraying.

4

How to Apply Gender Criticism to *Dirty Harry*

What Is Gender Criticism?

Gender criticism looks at the way gender is understood in a society. While *sex* is a biological label, *gender* refers to the roles men and women play in society, or their social performances. Society informs the expectations people have for male and female gender roles. Masculinity and femininity are social performances that combine psychology, behaviors, mannerisms, clothing, appearance, speech, and other factors.

Gender critics explore the way gender roles are presented in a work. They look at the elements of a performance that create a masculine or feminine perception. They also judge how these performances fit social expectations. Film is especially interesting because actors are giving actual performances.

Applying Gender Criticism to *Dirty Harry*

In *Dirty Harry*, police inspector Harry Callahan exaggerates the social expectations of masculinity. Furthermore, Eastwood is an actor famous for his recurring role as a Western cowboy, an undeniable symbol of masculinity. Eastwood transfers many of these masculine attributes to Callahan, playing him as a sort of urban cowboy. Callahan's representations of the male gender as hypermasculine illustrate the positive and negative effects imposed gender roles can have on a society.

Callahan is a deliberately exaggerated masculine stereotype. Callahan's gun is a .44 Magnum, "the most powerful handgun in the world," as he tells criminals.[1] Even though the gun is large and powerful, it has only six shots and sometimes leaves him defenseless. Callahan has chosen a gun that obviously

Thesis Statement

The author's thesis states: "Callahan's representations of the male gender as hypermasculine illustrate the positive and negative effects imposed gender roles can have on a society." The author spends the remainder of the essay discussing how Callahan's maleness reflects the impact of gender roles.

Argument One

The first argument provides evidence from the film that supports the first part of the thesis: "Callahan is a deliberately exaggerated masculine stereotype." The author examines how Callahan's character represents a stereotypical male.

represents masculinity because it is powerful and requires an operator who is brave enough to run out of shots, even though a different gun might serve him better.

Callahan also seems not to feel pain. When he is shot in the leg stopping a robbery early in the film, Callahan barely reacts to the injury and still manages to bring in one of the robbers. Further adding to his masculinity, Callahan has no domestic side. His wife is dead, he eats hot dogs outside and dines alone at burger joints, and he is never seen at home in the film. In contrast to his happily married

Unlike his new partner, Gonzalez, Callahan has no family or home life. This adds to his hypermasculinity.

partner, Chico Gonzalez, Callahan is married to his career.

Callahan serves the law, but the law is shown as feminized and ineffective. The chief of police brushes lint off his uniform, showing his preoccupation with his appearance. The mayor uses a gold-handled telephone. Because the law and its representatives are not masculine enough, Callahan acts out an extreme version of maleness to get the job done. He does not respect authority and breaks rules when needed to bring in Scorpio.

<u>Even Callahan shows awareness of his performance of maleness.</u> He says he has the nickname "Dirty" Harry because he gets "every dirty job that comes along."[2] The nickname has been imposed on him by others on the police force, but Callahan lives up to it. Callahan knowingly performs the role of surly, masculine cop. As the role demands, Callahan seems devoid of compassion. When a colleague says he is a bigot, hating everyone—African Americans, women, Hispanics—equally, Callahan agrees.

> **Argument Two**
> With the groundwork laid, the author moves to the second argument, which discusses Callahan's gender role as a performance: "Even Callahan shows awareness of his performance of maleness."

He adds "especially [Mexicans]" but then winks at DiGiorgio, indicating he is aware of the insensitivity of his statement to Gonzalez, a Hispanic man.[3]

Callahan again demonstrates a lack of compassion when he taunts the suicidal man on the roof. Callahan's words are so cruel that the man lunges at him, at which point Callahan knocks him out and saves his life. Though the audience may be surprised by the way the events unfold, Callahan is not. His exaggerated lack of compassion is clearly part of a planned performance.

<u>Although Callahan's hypermasculine, macho behavior is successful and effective at meeting social needs, it isolates him from society.</u> To catch the antisocial murderer, Callahan himself must become antisocial, operating outside the law. He defies the police chief repeatedly and tortures Scorpio to get information.

> **Argument Three**
> The third argument claims the results of Callahan's gender performance are positive for society but negative for him: "Although Callahan's hypermasculine, macho behavior is successful and effective at meeting social needs, it isolates him from society."

Callahan has no relationships with men or women. He has no social life, and he prefers to work alone, complaining when the captain assigns

Gonzalez as his partner. Callahan is successful at tracking and killing Scorpio. But he must do so alone and on his time off after the legal process blocks him. He doggedly trails Scorpio to prevent him from killing again. After finally killing Scorpio, Callahan throws away his badge. The act is symbolic of Callahan's rejection of the law and society's rejection of him.

Conclusion
The author's conclusion sums up the arguments and partially restates the thesis. The conclusion also leaves the reader with a new idea: Callahan's throwing away of his badge may illustrate that the benefits of hypermasculinity are not worth the cost.

Though Callahan's extreme portrayal of the male gender may seem to be the unintended consequence of a rough life, it becomes clear that Callahan himself is aware of his performance. His hypermasculine behavior helps him do his job effectively, but it also isolates him from society, showing the drawbacks of overly gendered behaviors. Callahan uses his masculinity for the greater good of society. However, in the end, he throws away his badge, a symbol of his masculinity, perhaps indicating that the rewards of stereotypically masculine behavior may not be worth the isolation.

Thinking Critically about *Dirty Harry*

Now it is your turn to assess the critique. Consider these questions:

1. The author asserts that Callahan's representation of maleness aids him in his job but isolates him from society. Do you agree? Why or why not?

2. What was the author's strongest argument? What was the weakest? What other evidence from the film could be used to support these arguments?

3. *Dirty Harry* was released in the 1970s. How might gender roles be portrayed differently if the movie were filmed today?

Other Approaches

The previous critique was just one possible way of applying gender criticism to *Dirty Harry*. A different gender critique might examine the way Callahan's character exhibits a type of hypermasculinity that supports negative masculine stereotypes. Yet another approach might take a closer look at the way Scorpio portrays the male gender.

Men Behaving Badly

Some critics have claimed that *Dirty Harry* simply celebrates the stereotype of men behaving badly and that the film yearns for a cowboy style of justice, where vigilantes take the law into their own hands. They argue that rather than asking questions about masculinity, Callahan's exuberant hypermasculinity is a form of wishful thinking.

A thesis statement examining these ideas could be: With his extreme masculine values and disregard for society's rules, the character Harry Callahan is a male fantasy reminiscent of the Western genre.

Scorpio's Gender Performance

Scorpio's masculinity is set up to be in direct contrast to Callahan's. Scorpio has long hair and wears effeminate clothing, including gloves and a peace-sign belt buckle. He laughs and squeals in an effeminate way. His character's portrayal of maleness feels unnatural to the viewer and underscores his role as the film's antagonist.

A thesis statement considering these ideas could be: Scorpio's nontraditional performance of the male gender makes him more unsettling to the viewer than a stereotypical masculine antagonist.

Eastwood plays Preacher in *Pale Rider*, a film he starred in and directed.

5

An Overview of *Pale Rider*

Pale Rider is set in Carbon Canyon, a small gold-panning community in California. Coy LaHood, the head of a large mining company, wants to start his own mining operation where the community is currently mining. LaHood sends a group of thugs to attack the mining camp, trying to force the townspeople to give up their claims. His men ransack the camp, destroying tents and structures and shooting 14-year-old Megan Wheeler's dog before they ride away. As Megan buries her dog, she prays for a miracle. A strange man on horseback, played by Eastwood, rides toward town.

Hull Barrett, the leader of the Carbon Canyon miners, goes into the nearby town of LaHood to pick up supplies. On his way home, LaHood's men attack him. The stranger arrives and fights off LaHood's men. Hull invites his rescuer back to Carbon Canyon to stay at his home. As the stranger is washing up in Hull's cabin, Hull notices large scars on the stranger's back.

Megan's mother, Sarah, has been spending a lot of time with Hull, and she initially does not trust the stranger. The stranger comes to be known as Preacher because he wears the white collar of a preacher's uniform. He helps Hull find gold. To LaHood's despair, Carbon Canyon begins to flourish under Preacher's gentle guidance. Megan falls in love with Preacher and offers to be intimate with him. He gently refuses her offer.

Preacher negotiates a settlement for the miners that forces LaHood to offer a fair price for their claims. However, if the miners refuse the offer, LaHood has hired a marshal, Stockburn, to force them out. When Preacher presents LaHood's offer to the miners, many are tempted to accept. But Hull reminds the miners they came to Carbon Canyon not only to strike it rich but also to build a life. The miners vote to turn down LaHood's offer, knowing the decision means they will have to fight LaHood and Stockburn.

A Time for Guns

Preacher heads to LaHood's mining camp to deliver the message, taking his belongings with him. The community believes he has abandoned them to their fate. Preacher then rides to town, where he takes a key and retrieves a strongbox that holds guns. He exchanges them for his white preacher's collar.

Megan has borrowed Hull's horse to look for Preacher, and as she rides, she stops to look at LaHood's mining operation. His men use a mining technique of blasting water at the hillside. This type of mining is destroying the landscape. Megan says it "looks like hell."[1] LaHood's son, Josh, finds her watching the mining. He drags her off her horse and nearly rapes her. Just in time, Preacher arrives. When Josh reaches for his gun, Preacher shoots his hand. Preacher takes Megan back to Carbon Canyon.

Meanwhile, one Carbon Canyon miner, Spider Conway, strikes it rich. He takes his gold rock and his two sons to town, where LaHood is in a bar describing Preacher to Stockburn. The marshal tells LaHood that Preacher sounds a lot like a man Stockburn once knew—only that man is

Preacher rescues
Megan from
LaHood's son,
Josh.

dead. Spider taunts LaHood from outside the bar.
Stockburn walks outside, and his deputies toy with
Spider, shooting at his feet to make him dance.
When Spider moves to draw his gun, the deputies
kill him. Stockburn tells Spider's sons to take his
body back to Carbon Canyon and send Preacher to
them the next morning, or their community will be
destroyed.

That night, Sarah asks Preacher if he will leave
one day. When he confirms that he will, she says
she will stay in Carbon Canyon and marry Hull. She
asks Preacher who he is, and he tells her it is not
important. They spend the night together.

Apocalypse Redirected

The next morning, Preacher and Hull destroy LaHood's mining operation, blowing up the equipment. Preacher pretends to fumble dynamite, getting Hull off his horse to fix the problem. Then Preacher drives Hull's horse away, so Hull cannot follow him to town. Preacher intends to fight Stockburn and LaHood and does not want Hull to be hurt or killed. As he rides away, Preacher tells Hull to take care of Sarah and Megan.

In town, LaHood tells Stockburn Preacher has arrived. Preacher enters a shop where LaHood's men ambush him. But they are no match for Preacher. He shoots the men one at a time. Stockburn sees Preacher's face for the first time, crying "You!" as Preacher shoots him, creating a pattern of bullet holes in his chest that is nearly identical to the scars on Preacher's own body.[2] LaHood nearly shoots Preacher, but Hull has walked the long way to town and shoots LaHood just in time, rescuing Preacher. "Long walk," Preacher says to Hull before riding away.[3]

Megan rides to town to say good-bye to Preacher, but he has already ridden off toward the mountains as mysteriously as he came.

Aspects of Eastwood's character in *Pale Rider*, Preacher, can be found in many other narratives and stories.

How to Apply Archetypal Criticism to *Pale Rider*

What Is Archetypal Criticism?

Psychologist Carl Jung was the first to widely discuss archetypal theory and the collective unconscious—experiences and situations shared by all of humanity. Jung proposed a library of archetypes found even deeper than our unconscious. In archetypal criticism, the critic looks for similar images, symbols, characters, or plot structures that are found in narratives around the world. Archetypal criticism connects a specific work to a library of archetypes in human experience. Archetypes can also be found in symbols, settings, or specific characters, such as the hero, the goddess, and the mentor. Archetypes can also include types of narrative structures, including a hero's quest or a hero's return home.

Archetypal criticism is closely linked to myth criticism. Many myths from different cultures share the same archetypes. Fairy tales and folklore offer many different archetypal characters and structures; global religions also feature archetypes.

Applying Archetypal Criticism to *Pale Rider*

Death has been personified through many different myths and archetypes throughout human history. One death archetype, the image of death riding a pale horse, comes from the Bible. This image is from the book of Revelation, which concerns the apocalypse. The fourth horseman of the apocalypse represents this version of death.

Pale Rider makes the connection between the pale rider, Preacher, and death, the fourth horseman of the apocalypse, early in the film. Eastwood's Preacher represents the personification of death and shows humans must overcome their fear of death to succeed.

Thesis Statement

The author's essay discusses which archetype Preacher represents and the significance of this archetype's appearance in the film. The thesis states: "Eastwood's Preacher represents the personification of death and shows humans must overcome their fear of death to succeed."

The religious references in the film and the film's use of supernatural elements connect Preacher to death. At the beginning of the film, Megan prays for "a miracle" to help the Carbon Canyon miners survive the attacks by LaHood's men.[1] Using overlapping images of Megan praying, aerial shots swooping from the clouds toward the canyon, and views of the rider on the pale horse, the wish for a miracle and the arrival of Preacher are shown as a linked cause and effect. When Preacher arrives in Carbon Canyon, Megan is reading aloud from Revelation. Preacher is framed in the window as she reads about the fourth horseman.

As the film's title character, Preacher is not simply the rider of a pale horse, but a pale rider himself. Different occurrences throughout the film strongly suggest Preacher is, in fact, a ghost. Preacher arrives and leaves mysteriously, and no one ever learns his real name. When Sarah asks him, "Who are you, really?" he refuses to tell her.[2] Preacher also has a pattern of bullet-wound scars on

Argument One

The first argument lays the groundwork for the critique, showing the archetype is present in the film: "The religious references in the film and the film's use of supernatural elements connect Preacher to death." Without this argument, the rest of the critique would not be as clear.

his back, and the film suggests Stockburn put them there. When talking to LaHood, Stockburn thinks he recognizes Preacher from the description, but he says that man is dead. When Stockburn finally sees Preacher, his recognition of Preacher as the man he killed is obvious. Additionally, Preacher's aim with a gun is supernaturally perfect.

Argument Two

The second argument discusses Preacher's magnetism with the miners: "Despite his mysterious behavior, the Carbon Canyon residents grow to trust Preacher, indicating they have begun to accept the eventuality of death." This argument shows how the miners are growing closer to overcoming their fears of death.

Despite his mysterious behavior, the Carbon Canyon residents grow to trust Preacher, indicating they have begun to accept the eventuality of death. Although Sarah is initially wary of the stranger, both she and Megan come to admire him. Megan offers to be intimate with Preacher, confessing that she loves him. Although she did not trust him initially, Sarah warms up to Preacher. She kisses him, and they spend the night together. Later, she tells Megan, "He knows we both love him."[3] At the end of the film, Megan rides into town to tell Preacher good-bye. When she learns he has already left, she shouts into the mountains: "We all love you, Preacher. I love you!"[4]

The community also embraces Preacher, and he motivates the Carbon Canyon miners to take action. The community behaves differently with him among them. Instead of taking LaHood's monetary offer and protecting themselves, they vote to fight. Rather than simply acting as the gunslinging hand of fate, Preacher inspires the miners to take their fates into their own hands. He gives them a choice. They instinctively trust Preacher, asking his advice on whether they should take LaHood's deal, but he does not offer his opinion. The choice is the miners'

The Carbon Canyon miners, Megan and Sarah in particular, grow to trust Preacher and rely on his judgment.

Hull Barrett
leads the Carbon
Canyon miners
and eventually
rescues Preacher.

own. The film's early and later scenes in town show
Preacher's effect on the miners. Early in the film,
LaHood's men beat Hull, and Preacher rescues him.

In the final scene, Hull makes the "long walk" into town and shoots LaHood, rescuing Preacher.[5]

Their vote against LaHood's deal is a reflection of the Carbon Canyon miners overcoming their fear of death. Although the miners have the legal right to stay, they know they will be harmed and possibly killed if they do so. Thanks to Preacher, LaHood even makes them a fair offer. He will pay $1,000 to each miner for the Carbon Canyon claims. Despite this, Hull talks the miners out of selling their "dignity," though Sarah tells him it was foolish to do so.[6] For Hull, an honorable death is preferable to selling out. The fact that Preacher, personifying death, is shown to be a brave and honorable man further illustrates this idea.

> **Argument Three**
> The third argument ties the first two arguments together: "Their vote against LaHood's deal is a reflection of the Carbon Canyon miners overcoming their fear of death." The author asserts that because Preacher personifies death and the miners are drawn to and trust Preacher, they have embraced the idea of death.

If the community shows its acceptance of death by summoning Preacher, the end still turns out well. Preacher destroys LaHood's gang, his mining operation, and the threat of Stockburn's hired guns. The community is stronger than ever, having banded together, and of all the miners, only Hull has a death on his hands at the end of the film. This ending for the community shows that embracing the possibility of death is a positive act.

Conclusion

The last paragraph is the conclusion to the essay. The conclusion partially restates the thesis, now backed up by the author's supporting arguments.

The plot of *Pale Rider* is a familiar one in Western films. It features action, violence, and a community that takes a stand when threatened by corrupt forces. However, the unusual use of the biblical archetype in *Pale Rider* to express death makes an interesting contrast to the typical Western. The supernatural and biblical elements throughout the film draw the viewer, like the Carbon Canyon miners, to Preacher. When the Carbon Canyon miners finally embrace death, personified by Eastwood's Preacher, they are able to beat LaHood and his men, showing that though humans may naturally fear death, they must overcome this fear to thrive.

Thinking Critically about *Pale Rider*

Now it is your turn to assess the critique. Consider these questions:

1. The author argues that by embracing Preacher and his personification of death, the Carbon Canyon miners are able to defeat LaHood. Do you agree? Why or why not?

2. Are there any other archetypes that can be found in Preacher's character?

3. The author's conclusion should summarize the arguments, restate the thesis, and leave the reader with a new idea. Does this conclusion do so effectively? Why or why not?

Other Approaches

There are countless archetypes and many different ways to apply archetypal criticism to a work; the previous critique was just one approach. Another archetypal critique of *Pale Rider* might discuss the ways in which Preacher is representative of the anti-apocalypse. A different critique might examine the heroic journey the Carbon Canyon miners undertake after meeting Preacher.

The Anti-Apocalypse

A different approach using the archetype of death on a pale horse could argue Eastwood's Preacher is not ushering in the end of the world at all but rather helping the human community learn to protect itself against the apocalypse. This is a twist on what the audience expects from the death archetype.

A thesis discussing this idea could be: In *Pale Rider*, Preacher does not bring in the apocalypse but helps the mining community avert it. One argument could discuss the fact that Preacher only fights when attacked and how he does not fetch his guns from their strongbox until after Stockburn has been sent for and community members fear for their lives. Preacher kills nobody until the final shootout with Stockburn and his men. However, Preacher's presence gives the miners the courage to stand up for themselves against LaHood and his men.

Hull Barrett's Journey

As the Carbon Canyon miners' leader, Hull is very similar to Preacher. Still, at the beginning of the film, Hull is not able to inspire or protect the miners in the way Preacher does once he arrives. The arrival of Preacher acts as a catalyst for Hull, allowing him to undergo a heroic journey that prepares him to effectively lead his community. By the end of the film, Hull saves Preacher and his community when he shoots LaHood.

A thesis further considering these ideas could be: The arrival of Preacher instigates Hull Barrett's heroic journey, which leads him to become a powerful leader of his community.

Eastwood both directed *Unforgiven* and starred in the film, playing retired outlaw William Munny.

7

An Overview
of *Unforgiven*

Unforgiven takes place in Big Whiskey, Wyoming,
in the year 1880. When Delilah, a prostitute at a
local saloon, insults outlaw Quick Mike, he cuts her
face with his knife. Big Whiskey's sheriff, Little
Bill Daggett, orders Quick Mike and Davey to
give seven horses to Skinny, the saloon owner, as
payment. The other prostitutes in the saloon, furious
at this injustice, set a bounty. Whoever kills the two
cowboys for them will get $1,000.

The young Schofield Kid aims to win the
bounty, but he needs the help of a seasoned killer
to do it. He approaches William Munny, played
by Eastwood, who is living in Kansas. Munny is
a reformed outlaw and widower trying to run a
hog farm with his two children. His wife died two
years ago. Munny tells the Kid he is through with

the gunslinging life and sends him away. However, Munny's farm is failing. He eventually saddles up and leaves his children, saying he will be back in two weeks. Before catching up with the Kid, Munny persuades his old friend Ned Logan to join him.

Ned and Munny soon catch up with the Kid. Although the Kid brags to them that he has killed five men, his sight is extremely poor. He nearly shoots Munny and Ned as they catch up to him. The Kid is angry Ned has come, but Munny will not stay without him.

The Sheriff Sends a Message

In Big Whiskey, the sheriff learns about the bounty. He worries gunslingers will come to town seeking the bounty and will bring trouble with them. Little Bill enforces complete gun control in the town of Big Whiskey. All guns must be turned in to his office whenever travelers arrive in town.

English Bob is the first to come to town in pursuit of the bounty. When Little Bill realizes Bob has not turned in his guns, he brutally beats him and takes him to jail. Little Bill says he is sending a message with the beating: no others should come to Big Whiskey looking for the bounty.

When Munny, Ned, and the Kid arrive, they head straight for the saloon. Ned and the Kid go upstairs to meet the prostitutes while Munny waits for them in the bar below. Little Bill spots Munny and, correctly assuming he is after the bounty, beats him. Upstairs, Ned and the Kid escape through a window and find Munny in the street, seriously injured. They help him get out of town, where Ned can take care of him. Munny contracts a serious fever and is too sick to travel. Eventually, Munny recovers, and he, Ned, and the Kid set off to find and kill the two cowboys.

Munny convinces his friend Ned Logan, *center*, to join him and the Kid, *left*, in the hunt for Quick Mike.

Contract Killings

The three first find Quick Mike's friend Davey with a group of other cowboys. Munny's group ambushes Davey, and Munny shoots him. Davey's death is slow, and his pleas for water torment Munny and Ned. Munny calls to the cowboys who were with Davey, promising not to shoot them if they give Davey a drink. They do, and Munny does not shoot. Ned abandons the mission and says he is going home. On Ned's way home, Little Bill's men capture him and take him into town, where he is questioned and brutally whipped.

Munny and the Kid continue their hunt for Quick Mike without Ned. They wait outside the house where Quick Mike is hiding, knowing he will eventually have to use the outhouse. When Quick Mike comes outside, the Kid shoots and kills him. After the killing, the Kid tearfully confesses he has never killed anyone before. Munny tells him: "It's a hell of a thing, killing a man."[1] He gives the Kid whiskey to calm his nerves, but it does not work.

When Delilah brings the bounty payment to their meeting place, the two men learn Little Bill has killed Ned. Munny sends the Kid away with the money and instructions to leave his and Ned's shares of the money to Munny's children. Then Munny rides toward Big Whiskey.

Violence Leads to Violence

A storm is raging as Munny arrives in Big Whiskey. Outside the saloon, he sees Ned's body displayed along with a sign stating Ned's fate will be the fate of all assassins. Munny enters the saloon and shoots Skinny. Little Bill instructs his men to shoot as soon as Munny has fired his second bullet. Munny's gun jams, but he still manages to shoot Little Bill and kill many others in the bar. He then orders anyone who does not want to die to leave the bar, and they do. Munny hears a pistol cock, and he realizes Little Bill is still alive. Munny steps on Little Bill's hand in time to stop him from shooting. Munny kills Little Bill and shoots another wounded man on his way out the door. He orders the townspeople to give Ned a proper burial and not to harm the prostitutes, or he will return and kill them all.

The epilogue, in the form of text on the screen, tells the viewer Munny and his children left Kansas. It is rumored they are living in San Francisco, California.

In *Unforgiven*, Munny has an extremely violent past.

8

How to Apply Moral Criticism to *Unforgiven*

What Is Moral Criticism?

Moral criticism focuses on themes of what is right and what is wrong. Whether an action is right or wrong is often determined by a society. Moral critics look at the way morality is presented in a film. They examine the characters to see if they subscribe to a particular moral code. Moral critics also consider a work's message and whether it advances or hinders a civilization. Some believe a work of art should teach as well as entertain. Moral criticism employs this belief when discussing works of art. For example, works are considered more valuable if they have messages about tolerance and social justice. Behind this belief is another: humans can improve their humanity through moral learning.

Applying Moral Criticism to *Unforgiven*

Unforgiven, from its title to its main themes, invites the viewer to consider the ethics of violence. Westerns typically do not question the use of violence. However, in *Unforgiven*, the characters openly discuss the topic. Because of the unusual treatment of this topic in a Western, the film's audience is drawn into the discussion as well.

The director, Eastwood, agrees that the film has more to say than a regular Western on the topic of violence. Actor Gene Hackman was troubled by the violence of Westerns and had to be persuaded to play the violent role of Little Bill. Eastwood convinced him by saying the film could show "the moral implications of violence."[1] Eastwood meant violence hurts more than just the immediate victim and ultimately destroys those who use it on others. *Unforgiven* features the frequent violence of a traditional Western. But it shows the violence in a different light. For all its violence and gunplay, *Unforgiven* promotes an antiviolent message.

Thesis Statement

The author's thesis states: "For all its violence and gunplay, *Unforgiven* promotes an antiviolent message." The essay focuses on how the contradiction between the film's violent themes and its nonviolent message reveals itself.

Unforgiven adheres to the typical Western genre in that it has a great deal of violence and killing. Eastwood agrees with critics that "Western stories have always been built around violent behavior," and his own many previous Westerns prove the point.[2] *Unforgiven* conforms to the expectations of a traditional Western in many respects. For one, the story of *Unforgiven* is founded on vengeance, the ethics of which are rarely questioned in the typical Western film.

> **Argument One**
>
> The first argument discusses the ways in which *Unforgiven* is similar to a typical Western. The first argument states: "*Unforgiven* adheres to the typical Western genre in that it has a great deal of violence and killing." This sets up the arguments that follow.

The film's action is instigated by an act of violence with Quick Mike's attack on Delilah. When the prostitutes do not get justice from the sheriff, they seek vengeance by placing a bounty on Quick Mike and Davey. Quick Mike's initial act of violence creates more violence when Little Bill beats English Bob, who comes to town in pursuit of the bounty. Even Munny, a reformed gunslinger, is motivated back to his violent tendencies by vengeance. When Little Bill kills Ned, Munny ruthlessly kills anyone who stands in his way at the town saloon. The events set in motion by Quick Mike's attack on Delilah begin a cycle of violence that proves to be unstoppable.

However, *Unforgiven* is not a typical Western because many of the characters who commit violence are tormented by it. Ned, who, like Munny, is known for his violent past, is extremely troubled when Munny shoots Davey. Davey does not immediately die from his gunshot wounds and cries out for water until Munny shouts to Davey's companions to give the dying man a drink. Davey's death is shown as slow and pitiful. Ned cannot bring himself to finish off Davey, seeming to fall apart at this murder. Unable to handle the reality of violence, Ned abandons the mission.

> **Argument Two**
> The second argument begins discussing the contradiction in the film: "However, *Unforgiven* is not a typical Western because many of the characters who commit violence are tormented by it." The author claims it is not the amount of violence but the nature of it that is unusual in this Western.

The Kid, too, glorifies violence before his own act of murder. To him, killing a man is only a big event because there is a large bounty. He has heard Munny used to be a "cold-blooded assassin."[3] Now, he says, Munny no longer looks like a mean cowboy but a poor farmer. The Kid brags that he has killed five men, and as the men make camp, the Kid wants to hear about Munny's exploits. However, after actually killing Quick Mike, the Kid breaks down in tears. Again, the shooting is grotesque and pitiful. Quick Mike is shot while sitting on the latrine. The Kid turns to alcohol to blunt his pain and guilt over his act of murder. But the alcohol does not work, and the Kid is undone by his act of violence. The film suggests Munny's own drinking and his blurred memory are also the result of guilt over his former violent lifestyle.

Other acts of violence in *Unforgiven* are equally brutal, and the characters react accordingly to the brutality. One character urinates on himself when a gun is pointed at him. Little Bill's beating of English Bob is shown in enough detail to make the audience uncomfortable. Later, as Little Bill is beating Munny, Munny picks up a bottle from the bar, a typical bar brawl move in Western films. However, Munny fails to hit Little Bill with the bottle. Instead, he leaves the bar on his stomach, slowly crawling

> **Argument Three**
> The third argument goes into a deeper examination of the acts of violence in the film: "Other acts of violence in *Unforgiven* are equally brutal, and the characters react accordingly to the brutality."

out as the camera tracks him along the floor. He then slides down the steps into the mud.

Little Bill's whipping of Ned is so brutal even the men who are watching it wince and seem horrified. Although Little Bill has lost much sympathy by the end of the film, his final moments at the mercy of born-again killer Munny are also horrifying. The violence is not stylized, as in many Western films, to make it less grotesque. The camera lingers on the graphic and realistic details.

Although Munny commits the violence needed to avenge Delilah and Ned, he recognizes such violence is morally wrong. Munny is a reformed gunslinger. Although his past is only alluded to, the audience knows he was once an extremely violent man. Ned tells him, "you was one crazy son of a [gun], Will."[4]

Although Munny has put that life behind him, he is still haunted by his past actions. After Little Bill beats him, Munny suffers from a fever and comes close to dying. At this point, he tells Ned and the Kid he has nightmares; he sees

> **Argument Four**
>
> The fourth argument focuses on Munny's acts of violence: "Although Munny commits the violence needed to avenge Delilah and Ned, he recognizes such violence is morally wrong." The author argues that no matter the reasoning behind the violence, Munny remains a condemned man.

a grisly vision of his wife, her face crawling with worms. He is scared to die and says so several times.

At the end of the film as Munny is about to shoot and kill Little Bill, the sheriff says to him, "I'll see you in Hell, William Munny."[5] Munny answers, "Yeah," and kills Little Bill.[6] Munny believes he is damned. Even though he has used violence to avenge Delilah's injuries and Ned's death, Munny recognizes this avenging violence cannot make up for his past atrocities. Killing for vengeance is still an immoral act. Instead of

Although Munny kills Little Bill, seemingly ending the cycle of violence started when Delilah was attacked, Munny does not seem at peace as the film ends.

redeeming the hero, as a traditional Western usually does, Munny seems condemned.

Munny has the audience's sympathies because his farm is failing, his wife has died, and he has two children to support. He is a loyal friend to Ned and protects the Kid. Throughout the film, he only kills for a reason, whether it is to earn a bounty his children need or to avenge his friend. Still, Munny's acts of violence and the other acts of violence in the film are shown as brutal. The committers of violence are often torn apart by their acts, and the witnesses are troubled. The film uses the techniques of a traditional Western to argue violence is complicated and destructive. Although the film's hero, Munny, has escaped death, he suffers a moral sentence. At the end of film, Munny remains unforgiven.

> **Conclusion**
>
> The conclusion is the final paragraph of the critique. The author sums up the supporting arguments and partially restates the thesis. The author finishes the essay with a final point tying the critique to the film's title: "Munny remains unforgiven."

Thinking Critically about *Unforgiven*

Now it is your turn to assess the critique. Consider these questions:

1. The author asserts that *Unforgiven* uses violence to preach a message of nonviolence. Could the film have gotten this message across without showing violence? Would the message have been as effective? Why or why not?

2. Which of the arguments was the most convincing? Which was the weakest? What other evidence from the film could be used to support the author's thesis?

3. The author argues that *Unforgiven* takes a stance against violence. Does the film take a moral stance on any other topics?

Other Approaches

There are many different ways to apply moral criticism to a work. The previous essay was one example of a moral critique of *Unforgiven*. The essay focused on ethics in relation to violence. However, many moral critics use religion in their critiques, and this tactic could by applied to *Unforgiven* as well. Another approach could discuss the way the violence in *Unforgiven* illustrates the characters' devolution to animal tendencies.

Tackling Religion

Little Bill's promise to Munny, "I'll see you in Hell," raises the issue of religion in *Unforgiven*.[7] The eye-for-an-eye vision of justice exhibited in the film also comes from the Old Testament of the Bible. However, aside from these points, there are very few religious references in the film. The saloon doubles as a brothel. No church or religious figure is shown in the film. What does this lack of religion say about frontier justice and the situations in which the film's characters find themselves?

A thesis examining these ideas might be: Without religion or a clear moral path to follow, the flawed humans in *Unforgiven* must struggle with muddy definitions of right and wrong.

Reverting to Animal Nature

If moral criticism typically focuses on a belief that humanity can raise itself up and evolve positively, a film can also be used to make the opposite case. English Bob is a representative of civilized England. He speaks with an upper-class English accent and mocks the Americans for not having a king or queen. However, this attitude is short-lived. English Bob's exploits are proved to be lies and fabrications. As he leaves Big Whiskey, he shouts abuse in a lower-class English accent. Munny considers himself a reformed killer until he gets back on a horse and rides out to kill a man. Additionally, Little Bill represents law and order in Big Whiskey, but he is obviously a cruel and violent man.

A thesis statement further examining these ideas could be: The extreme violence in *Unforgiven* illustrates that though humanity might try to raise itself up, violence is its natural instinct.

Frankie Dunn, played by Eastwood, has trained many boxers, but his overcautious approach holds back his fighters.

Chapter

9

An Overview of
Million Dollar Baby

Frankie Dunn, played by Eastwood, is a veteran
of the boxing world. He now runs a boxing gym,
the Hit Pit, as an owner and trainer. Frankie is a
good but extremely careful trainer. He feels guilty
because 25 years ago he did not stop the fighter he
was training from fighting in a match Frankie knew
he would lose. The fighter, Eddie "Scrap-Iron"
Dupris, known as Scrap, lost an eye in the fight
and had to retire. Scrap has remained friends with
Frankie and works at his gym.

Maggie Fitzgerald is a waitress who wants to
become a boxer. She asks Frankie to train her, but
he turns her down, telling her he does not train girls
and "tough ain't enough."[1] Maggie shows up at the
Hit Pit anyway, hassling Frankie to help her. She
saves her money to pay six months' dues at the gym

and trains relentlessly on her own. Scrap gives her some tips and a speed bag to help her train. Frankie gives her no encouragement.

Maggie's Rise to Fame

On the night of her thirty-second birthday, Maggie confronts Frankie. She has had a difficult life, and her family offers her no support. Her father is dead, her mother does not seem to care about her, her sister runs a welfare scam, and her brother is in prison. Maggie tells Frankie she has pulled herself out of a life that always threatens to pull her back. If she did not have boxing, she would have nothing at all. Seeing her passion, Frankie reluctantly begins giving her boxing tips, and they make a deal that he will become her trainer.

As Maggie improves, she begins asking when she can fight. Frankie says he will only train her, not manage her, and he sends her to a manager who puts her in a fight beyond her level. But seeing she is being hurt in the ring, Frankie coaches Maggie to win the fight. She makes him promise not to leave her again. Frankie will now manage and train Maggie. When she begins fighting under Frankie's supervision, she wins every match.

The audience learns Frankie has a daughter to
whom he writes every week. The letters always
come back unopened. The relationship between
Frankie and Maggie grows into mutual affection.
Maggie takes Frankie to a diner her father used to
take her to. Frankie likes the diner and the lemon
pie he orders, and he tells Maggie he might like to
own the diner some day.

Frankie sets Maggie up with a fight against a
British champion. Frankie gives her a silk robe with
the Gaelic phrase *Mo Cuishle* on the back. Maggie
does not know what the phrase means, and Frankie

As Frankie
coaches Maggie,
the two grow
closer and
establish a
relationship
beyond that
of trainee and
trainer, similar
to a father and
daughter.

does not tell her, but the crowd loves the phrase and chants it during the fight. Maggie wins the fight and tours Europe with Frankie, fighting in boxing matches and continuing to improve.

After turning down offers for several big fights, Frankie accepts a fight for Maggie against Billie "the Blue Bear," a female boxer known for fighting dirty. Maggie will be rewarded $1 million if she wins. Maggie starts out strong and is winning the match until she turns her back on her opponent once the bell rings. Billie punches her hard, knocking Maggie out. As she falls, Maggie hits a stool put in the corner for her, even as Frankie tries to move it out of the way. She breaks her neck on the stool and is paralyzed.

The Lost Dream

Frankie stays by Maggie throughout her hospitalization. He blames himself for her injury. When Maggie gets bedsores, her legs must be amputated. She asks Frankie to help her to die, so she can go out fighting. Frankie refuses, and Maggie bites her own tongue, hoping to bleed to death. She continues trying to hurt herself until she is kept sedated.

Frankie realizes how desperate Maggie has become and begins contemplating helping her. One night, Frankie packs a bag and visits Maggie. He finally tells her the Gaelic phrase means "my darling, my blood."[2] He turns off her respirator and kills her with an injection of adrenaline.

Scrap narrates the rest of the story through a letter to Frankie's daughter. According to Scrap, Frankie has disappeared. The last shot of the film suggests he has gone to the diner where he and Maggie ate lemon pie.

Maggie meets her match when she fights Billie, a boxer known for her dirty fighting.

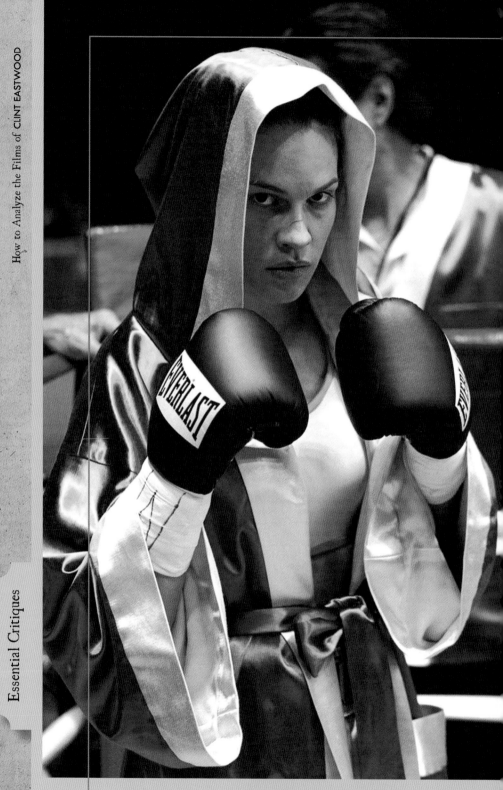

By succeeding in a traditionally masculine sport, Maggie Fitzgerald proves she is not a stereotypical female.

10

How to Apply Feminist Criticism to *Million Dollar Baby*

What Is Feminist Criticism?

Feminism asserts that women's rights and opportunities should be equal to those of men. Feminist criticism analyzes how works depict women and the roles and rights available to them in the time period in which the work is set. A critic does not need to be female to engage in feminist criticism. By considering the ways female characters work with or against society's expectations of them and how those expectations are represented, feminist critics can suggest whether the work itself is feminist or antifeminist.

Feminist critics believe most women exist in a patriarchal society where men are viewed as superior and therefore have more privileges. In feminist criticism, it is important to look at societal contexts such as this one. Feminist critics study the relationships between women and men, but these relationships can also be seen in a society's laws, politics, religions, and economics. Often, feminist critiques identify ways female characters overcome stereotypes and inequality in a patriarchal society.

Applying Feminist Criticism to *Million Dollar Baby*

There are very few women depicted in *Million Dollar Baby*, and boxing is shown to be a male sport. Frankie even says, "I don't train girls."[1] However, Maggie is not satisfied with the limiting female roles in her life. She works a dead-end job as a waitress, and her family is depicted as awful and does not appreciate her. Throughout the film, Maggie talks about boxing as her only escape from a limiting life. As a woman engaging in a traditionally male sport, Maggie's struggles illustrate the ways in which women are limited by traditional patriarchal structures.

> **Thesis Statement**
>
> The author's thesis states: "As a woman engaging in a traditionally male sport, Maggie's struggles illustrate the ways in which women are limited by traditional patriarchal structures." The remainder of the essay shows how Maggie is restricted in the male-dominated sport of boxing.

Frankie's attitudes toward training women initially keep Maggie from success. Overcoming Frankie's resistance to training a woman is the first struggle Maggie must face in pursuing her boxing dreams. Although Maggie has talent and grit, she makes no progress in boxing on her own until Frankie agrees to be her trainer. Maggie seeks out Frankie and tirelessly insists he trains her. Frankie points out more than once that there are plenty of other trainers out there who work with women, but Maggie believes he is the best and will not settle for less. Maggie has spent three years training on her own, and she recognizes that she needs a professional to improve.

Frankie's comments show he has no respect for women. He is initially adamant against training her. He calls her "Girlie," telling her, "Tough ain't enough."[2] When Frankie finally agrees to be her trainer, he expects her to cry when he gives her boxing advice. But Maggie is more determined than he is. She agrees she does not want or expect any special treatment as a woman. When she is injured,

> **Argument One**
> The first argument states: "Frankie's attitudes toward training women initially keep Maggie from success." The author discusses Frankie's negative attitude toward women and how Maggie overcomes this obstacle.

she insists on continuing a fight even though Frankie wants her to stop. She proves equal to men in the typically male-dominated sport. However, Frankie continues holding her back when he tries to protect her from being hurt.

By succeeding in boxing, Maggie escapes her limiting family roles. However, her relationship with Frankie resembles that of a patriarchal father-daughter relationship. Maggie's mother is a widow, her sister has a welfare scam, and her brother is in prison. Maggie fears becoming like the rest of her family. She explains this to Frankie on the night he agrees to train her.

> **Argument Two**
>
> The author's second argument discusses Maggie's family and the patriarchal structure that forms in the relationship she establishes with Frankie. The second argument states: "By succeeding in boxing, Maggie escapes her limiting family roles. However, her relationship with Frankie resembles that of a patriarchal father-daughter relationship."

Maggie's father died when she was a child, but in Frankie, Maggie finds a father figure and someone who cares about her. Frankie, too, begins viewing Maggie as a daughter. Although he does not tell her what it means, the writing on Maggie's robe, translating to "my darling, my blood," proves Frankie's feelings toward her.[3] When Maggie

is hospitalized, her biological family shows little concern, while Frankie stays with Maggie throughout her ordeal. He eventually ends Maggie's life as she has begged him to, even though it is emotionally difficult for him to do so, showing the depth of his feelings for her. Maggie's relationship with Frankie is portrayed as positive but stays within the confines of a traditional father-daughter relationship. Frankie mentors and protects Maggie, helping her to succeed. In the end, she is unable to achieve her goal of taking her life without Frankie's

As Maggie and Frankie grow closer, she begins viewing him as a father figure.

help. Maggie is never able to stand completely on her own.

Argument Three

The last argument deals with Maggie's disablement in the ring: "The outcome of Maggie's success as a boxer indicates that successful women become targets for other women." The author argues that Maggie's paralysis seems to be a punishment for success and notices that another woman inflicts the injury.

The outcome of Maggie's success as a boxer indicates that successful women become targets for other women. Maggie's final fight is with Billie "the Blue Bear," a woman who is overly aggressive and fights dirty. After Maggie turns the fight and begins dominating, Billie hits her after the bell has rung. This punch results in Maggie breaking her neck on the stool. The act implies that Billie feels threatened by Maggie. Billie's masculine characterization and the fact that the male referee, although cautioning her, does not disqualify her for her dirty fighting, supports the argument that patriarchal culture encourages women to target other women.

As if to punish her for her aspirations to greatness, Maggie is permanently disabled in the ring. However, rather than accept even tighter limitations on her freedom and future, she chooses to "fight her way out" of life.[4] As in the beginning,

she must overcome Frankie's resistance to helping her. Again, through determination she succeeds. Because of the parallel to this pattern at the beginning, the film presents Maggie's death as a form of triumph. She chooses to live on her own

Maggie relies on Frankie's coaching in many aspects of her life, not just boxing.

terms, with Frankie's help, and she chooses to die on her own terms, with Frankie's help.

> **Conclusion**
> The conclusion is the final paragraph of the critique. It summarizes the author's main points and partially restates the thesis. The conclusion also leaves the reader with a new thought, explaining that although Maggie fulfilled her dream of becoming a boxer, she had to do it on the patriarchal terms of the boxing world.

With its main character, Maggie Fitzgerald, overcoming many obstacles to succeed in a male-dominated sport, *Million Dollar Baby* shows that women can succeed in a patriarchal society. However, the struggles Maggie faces as she tries to make it as a boxer underscore the issues women face in such a society. Women can triumph, but they must overcome social obstacles set in place by patriarchy to do so. Additionally, Maggie is able to succeed only with the help of a male, Frankie. Even though Maggie fulfilled her dream of becoming a boxer, she must do so on the terms of the patriarchal boxing community, and the fulfillment of this dream ultimately leads to her death.

Thinking Critically about *Million Dollar Baby*

Now it is your turn to assess the critique. Consider these questions:

1. The author's thesis states that Maggie's struggle to become a boxer illustrates the struggles women face in a patriarchal society. What other evidence from the film supports this idea? Is there any evidence that disputes it?

2. Frankie cannot mend the relationship with his actual daughter, despite evidence that he writes to her every week. How does his relationship with his daughter change the relationship between him and Maggie?

3. Frankie says he does not train girls, and Maggie says she does not want Frankie to treat her any differently because she is a woman. Do you think Frankie treats her in the same way he would a male boxer? Why or why not?

Other Approaches

You just read one possible feminist critique of *Million Dollar Baby*. However, there are many different ways to apply feminist criticism to a work. Another feminist critique of *Million Dollar Baby* could discuss the ways in which the film is antifeminist by focusing on the character of Frankie. Yet another critique could focus on the sport of female boxing and the way it pits women against each other as opponents.

An Antifeminist Film

Maggie is Frankie's project. As her trainer, he has to break her down in order to build her up again. As a result, it could be argued that *Million Dollar Baby* is really a film about Frankie and not Maggie. Frankie owns the gym. Maggie calls him "boss."[5] Frankie's attitude toward women does not really improve but is instead transformed into fatherlike affection. Even the name Frankie gives Maggie is a claim to her, "my darling, my blood," therefore claiming her victories as his own.[6] At the end, Maggie is completely dependent on Frankie, and he even has power over whether she lives or dies. Essentially, the relationship has stayed the same throughout the film.

A thesis statement discussing these ideas could be: Maggie's total dependence on Frankie for her success promotes the idea that a strong woman must have a strong man supporting her.

Women against Women

Some feminist critiques look at the ways female relationships are portrayed in a work. Many feminist critics argue that women compete against each other for male attention. Maggie has no positive relationships with other females and few female relationships outside her family. Her most frequent contact with other women comes in the boxing ring, when they face as opponents.

A thesis statement further considering these ideas could be: *Million Dollar Baby* reinforces the idea that in a patriarchal society, women are in constant competition with each other.

You Critique It

Now that you have learned about several different critical theories and how to apply them to film, are you ready to perform a critique of your own? You have read that this type of evaluation can help you look at movies from a new perspective and make you pay attention to issues you may not have otherwise recognized. So, why not use one of the critical theories profiled in this book to consider a fresh take on your favorite movie?

First, choose a theory and the movie you want to analyze. Remember that the theory is a springboard for asking questions about the work.

Next, write a specific question that relates to the theory you have selected. Then you can form your thesis, which should provide the answer to that question. Your thesis is the most important part of your critique and offers an argument about the work based on the tenets, or beliefs, of the theory you are applying. Recall that the thesis statement typically appears at the very end of the introductory paragraph of your essay. It is usually only one sentence long.

After you have written your thesis, find evidence to back it up. Good places to start are in the work itself or journals or articles that discuss what other people have said about it. Since you are critiquing a movie, you may

also want to read about the director's life to get a sense
of what factors may have affected the creative process.
This can be useful if working within historical or auteur
types of criticism.

Depending on which theory you apply, you can often
find evidence in the movie's language, plot, or character
development. You should also explore parts of the movie
that seem to disprove your thesis and create an argument
against them. As you do this, you might want to address
what other critics have written about the movie. Their
quotes may help support your claim.

Before you start analyzing a work, think about the
different arguments made in this book. Reflect on how
evidence supporting the thesis was presented. Did you
find that some of the techniques used to back up the
arguments were more convincing than others? Try these
methods as you prove your thesis in your own critique.

When you are finished writing your critique, read it
over carefully. Is your thesis statement understandable?
Do the supporting arguments flow logically, with the
topic of each paragraph clearly stated? Can you add
any information that would present your readers with
a stronger argument in favor of your thesis? Were you
able to use quotes from the movie, as well as from other
critics, to enhance your ideas?

Did you see the work in a new light?

Timeline

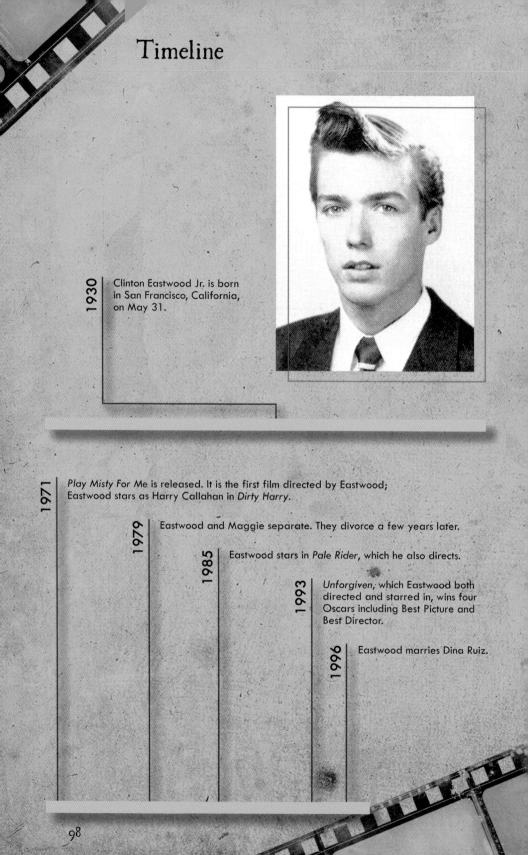

1930 — Clinton Eastwood Jr. is born in San Francisco, California, on May 31.

1971 — *Play Misty For Me* is released. It is the first film directed by Eastwood; Eastwood stars as Harry Callahan in *Dirty Harry*.

1979 — Eastwood and Maggie separate. They divorce a few years later.

1985 — Eastwood stars in *Pale Rider*, which he also directs.

1993 — *Unforgiven*, which Eastwood both directed and starred in, wins four Oscars including Best Picture and Best Director.

1996 — Eastwood marries Dina Ruiz.

1951 Eastwood is drafted for the Korean War.

1953 Eastwood marries Maggie Johnson on December 19.

1955 Eastwood makes his film debut with a minor role in *Revenge of the Creature*.

1959 The popular television series *Rawhide* begins airing with Eastwood in the role of Rowdy Yates.

1964 *A Fistful of Dollars* releases in Europe. It first of three spaghetti Westerns Eastwood will film with director Sergio Leone.

1966 *Rawhide*'s last episode airs.

1967 Eastwood forms his own production company.

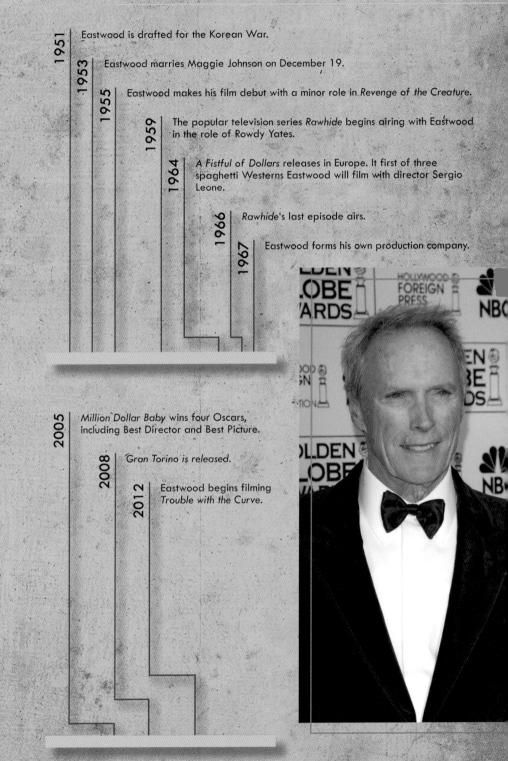

2005 *Million Dollar Baby* wins four Oscars, including Best Director and Best Picture.

2008 *Gran Torino* is released.

2012 Eastwood begins filming *Trouble with the Curve*.

Glossary

antagonist
> The character or force that opposes the hero or main character of a work.

apocalypse
> The end of the world.

catalyst
> An agent that encourages or causes change.

claim
> A piece of land that has been staked out as belonging to an individual.

drafted
> Selected for military service.

effeminate
> Stereotypically feminine, often used in a negative sense.

genre
> A category of film, literature, or other art characterized by a particular style, form, or content.

hypermasculine
> Exhibiting excessively masculine tendencies.

macho
Stereotypically masculine.

patriarchal
When a society or organization is mostly ruled by men.

personified
Represented something as a human.

production company
A company that oversees the creation of a film and handles production aspects, including the budget, scheduling, hiring, and more.

psychology
The science of the mind and behavior.

stereotype
An opinion about a person or group of people based on assumptions.

stylized
Represented by a particular style pattern rather than reality.

vigilantes
Self-appointed enforcers of the law who enact justice on their own terms.

Bibliography of Works and Criticism

Important Works

Rawhide, 1959–1966

A Fistful of Dollars, 1964

For a Few Dollars More, 1965

The Good, the Bad and the
Ugly, 1966

Where Eagles Dare, 1968

Dirty Harry, 1971

Play Misty for Me, 1971

Magnum Force, 1973

High Plains Drifter, 1973

The Outlaw Josey Wales, 1976

The Enforcer, 1976

Every Which Way But Loose,
1978

Escape from Alcatraz, 1979

Bronco Billy, 1980

Any Which Way You Can, 1980

Sudden Impact, 1983

Pale Rider, 1985

The Dead Pool, 1988

Bird, 1988

Unforgiven, 1992

The Bridges of Madison
County, 1995

Midnight in the Garden of
Good and Evil, 1997

Space Cowboys, 2000

Mystic River, 2003

Million Dollar Baby, 2004

Flags of Our Fathers, 2006

Letters from Iwo Jima, 2006

Gran Torino, 2008

Invictus, 2009

Hereafter, 2010

J. Edgar, 2011

Critical Discussions

Beard, William. *Persistence of Double Vision: Essays on Clint Eastwood*. Edmonton, AB: U of Alberta P, 2000. Print.

Bingham, Dennis. *Acting Male: Masculinities in the Films of James Stewart, Jack Nicholson, and Clint Eastwood*. New Brunswick, NJ: Rutgers, 1994. Print.

Cornell, Drucilla. *Clint Eastwood and Issues of American Masculinity*. New York: Fordham UP, 2009. Print.

Engel, Leonard, ed. *Clint Eastwood, Actor and Director: New Perspectives*. Salt Lake City, UT: U of Utah P, 2007. Print.

Knapp, Laurence F. *Directed by Clint Eastwood: Eighteen Films Analyzed*. Jefferson, NC: McFarland, 1996. Print.

Resources

Selected Bibliography

Avery, Kevin, ed. *Conversations with Clint: Paul Nelson's Lost Interviews with Clint Eastwood 1979–1983*. New York: Continuum, 2011. Print.

"Eastwood on Eastwood." Dir. Richard Schickel. 1997. *Unforgiven*. 1992. Warner Brothers, 2002. DVD.

Kapsis, Robert E., and Kathie Coblentz, eds. *Clint Eastwood: Interviews*. Jackson: UP of Mississippi, 1999. Print.

Pale Rider. Dir. Clint Eastwood. Warner Brothers, 1985. DVD.

Further Readings

Eliot, Marc. *American Rebel: The Life of Clint Eastwood*. New York: Harmony, 2009. Print.

Frangioni, David, and Thomas Schatz. *Clint Eastwood, Icon: The Essential Film Art Collection*. San Rafael, CA: Insight Editions, 2009. Print.

Schickel, Richard. *Clint Eastwood: A Biography*. New York: Knopf, 1996. Print.

Verlhac, Pierre-Henri. *Clint Eastwood: A Life in Pictures*. San Francisco: Chronicle, 2008. Print.

Web Links

To learn more about critiquing the films of Clint
Eastwood, visit ABDO Publishing Company online
at **www.abdopublishing.com**. Web sites about the films
of Clint Eastwood are featured on our Book Links page.
These links are routinely monitored and updated to
provide the most current information available.

For More Information

The Academy of Motion Picture Arts and Sciences
8949 Wilshire Boulevard, Beverly Hills, CA 90211
310-247-3000
www.oscars.org

The Academy of Motion Picture Arts and Sciences is the
organization responsible for selecting the nominees and
winners for the annual Academy Awards, or Oscars.

The California Museum: California Hall of Fame
1020 O Street, Sacramento, CA 95814
916-653-7524
www.californiamuseum.org

The California Museum recognizes Californians who
have had a positive influence on the state, the country,
and the world. Clint Eastwood was inducted into the
museum's Hall of Fame in 2006.

Source Notes

Chapter 1. Introduction to Critiques
None.

Chapter 2. A Closer Look at Clint Eastwood
　　1. Richard Schickel. *Clint Eastwood: A Biography*. New York: Knopf, 1996. Print. 46.
　　2. Clint Eastwood. Interview by Rex Reed, 1971. *Clint Eastwood: Interviews*. Eds. Robert E. Kapsis and Kathie Coblentz. Jackson: UP Mississippi, 1999. Print. 5.
　　3. Richard Schickel. *Clint Eastwood: A Biography*. New York: Knopf, 1996. Print. 232.
　　4. Ibid. 263.

Chapter 3. An Overview of *Dirty Harry*
　　1. *Dirty Harry*. Dir. Don Siegel. Warner Brothers, 1971. DVD.
　　2. Ibid.
　　3. Ibid.

Chapter 4. How to Apply Gender Criticism to *Dirty Harry*

1. *Dirty Harry*. Dir. Don Siegel. Warner Brothers, 1971. DVD.

2. Ibid.

3. Ibid.

Chapter 5. An Overview of *Pale Rider*

1. *Pale Rider*. Dir. Clint Eastwood. Warner Brothers, 1985. DVD.

2. Ibid.

3. Ibid.

Chapter 6. How to Apply Archetypal Criticism to *Pale Rider*

1. *Pale Rider*. Dir. Clint Eastwood. Warner Brothers, 1985. DVD.

2. Ibid.

3. Ibid.

4. Ibid.

5. Ibid.

6. Ibid.

Chapter 7. An Overview of *Unforgiven*

1. *Unforgiven*. Dir. Clint Eastwood. Warner Brothers, 1992. DVD.

Chapter 8. How to Apply Moral Criticism to *Unforgiven*

1. Clint Eastwood. Interview by Henri Béhar. 1992. *Clint Eastwood: Interviews*. Eds. Robert E. Kapsis and Kathie Coblentz. Jackson: UP of Mississippi, 1999. Print. 189.

2. Clint Eastwood. Interview by Thierry Jousee and Camille Nevers. 1992. *Clint Eastwood: Interviews*. Eds. Robert E. Kapsis and Kathie Coblentz. Jackson: UP of Mississippi, 1999. Print. 177.

3. *Unforgiven*. Dir. Clint Eastwood. Warner Brothers, 1992. DVD.

4. Ibid.

5. Ibid.

6. Ibid.

7. Ibid.

Chapter 9. An Overview of *Million Dollar Baby*

1. *Million Dollar Baby*. Dir. Clint Eastwood. Warner Brothers, 2004. DVD.

2. Ibid.

Chapter 10. How to Apply Feminist Criticism *Million Dollar Baby*

1. *Million Dollar Baby*. Dir. Clint Eastwood. Warner Brothers, 2004. DVD.

2. Ibid.

3. Ibid.

4. Ibid.

5. Ibid.

6. Ibid.

Index

About the Author

Casie Hermansson, PhD, teaches literature and film, two of her passions, at Pittsburg State University in Kansas. She has published fiction, poetry, and essays for younger readers in magazines in the United States and Australia.

Photo Credits

Featureflash/Shutterstock Images, cover, 3, 12, 99; Seth Poppel/Yearbook Library, 15, 98; Bob Galbraith/AP Images, 23; Everett Collection, 24, 35, 66, 73; Warner Brothers/ Photofest, 27, 32; Mary Evans/Ronald Grant/Everett Collection, 31; Warner Bros./Everett Collection, 42, 46, 53, 54, 60, 63, 81, 83, 84, 89; Mary Evans/Warner Bros./Ronald Grant/Everett Collection, 48, 78; Merie W. Wallace/Warner Bros. Entertainment Inc./Photofest, 91